DECORATIVE PATTERNS FROM HISTORIC SOURCES

Edited by James Spero

Dover Publications, Inc., New York

Publisher's Note

The tremendous technological advances of the nineteenth century made it possible to produce goods and materials for a market far wider than had existed previously. Most products needed the application of surface decoration. Designers turned to the past for inspiration, and by the 1850s a staggering variety of historical styles was being applied to all sorts of domestic and commercial goods. It was only later in the century that an attempt was made to evolve a coherent aesthetic of design.

Designers had constant resort to stylebooks, produced in great number, that contained page after page of line illustrations documenting as great a variety of art and architecture as possible. The present volume consists of a selection from one such book, *Flat Ornament: A Pattern Book of Designs of Textiles, Embroideries, Wall Papers, Inlays &c.* While the artwork is of superior quality, the identifications of many items are, unfortunately, incomplete. Nevertheless, as with the better examples of this genre, the book retains its intended use as a reference providing material as a source of ideas or for direct imitation.

Copyright © 1986 by Dover Publications, Inc.
All rights reserved under Pan American and International Copyright Conventions.

Published in Canada by General Publishing Company, Ltd., 30 Lesmill Road, Don Mills, Toronto, Ontario.
Published in the United Kingdom by Constable and Company, Ltd.

Decorative Patterns from Historic Sources is a new selection of plates from *Flat Ornament: A Pattern Book of Designs of Textiles, Embroideries, Wall Papers, Inlays &c.*, n.d., as printed at Stuttgart for J. Engelhorn and sold by B. T. Batsford, London.

DOVER *Pictorial Archive* SERIES

Manufactured in the United States of America
Dover Publications, Inc., 31 East 2nd Street, Mineola, N.Y. 11501

Library of Congress Cataloging-in-Publication Data
Main entry under title:

Decorative patterns from historic sources.

(Dover design library)
1. Decoration and ornament—Themes, motives. I. Spero, James. II. Series.
NK1530.D4 1986   745.4   86-436
ISBN 0-486-25120-9

Pattern of hangings from the Mantegna Hall in the Castello di Corte, Mantua.

Intarsia ornaments.

Pattern for wallpaper.

Textiles from fifteenth-century paintings and altar shrines.

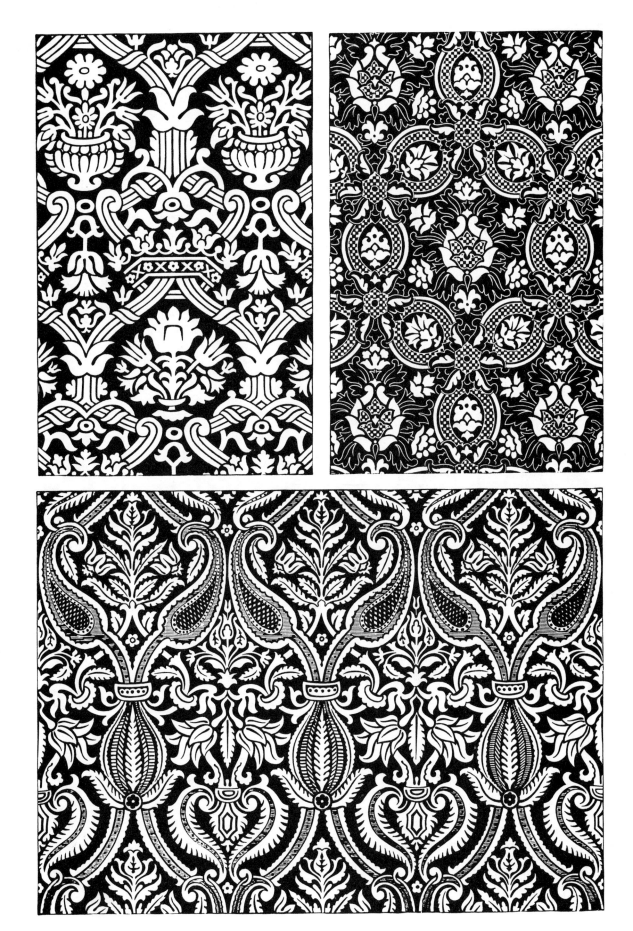

Sixteenth-century textile patterns.

Ornamental designs by the painter E. Charton, Paris.

Ornaments in stamped leather from bookbindings, Breslau (now Wrocław).

Medieval floor tiles.

German floor tiles.

Tablecloth.

German floor tiles.

Tablecloth.

Pattern for damask napkin.

Surface ornaments from buildings of the Italian Renaissance.

Borders from the marble floor of the Cathedral, Siena, fourteenth to sixteenth centuries.

Motifs from bookbindings and etched caskets.

Inlaid wood ornaments.

Mosaics, San Marco, Venice, end of the eleventh century.

Intarsia designs from seats, Sta. Maria dei Frari, Venice, fifteenth century.

17

Ornamental designs by Friedrich Fischbach (1839–1908).

Ornamental details from stalls, Monza.

Sixteenth-century wall painting, Trausnitz Castle, Landshut, Bavaria.

Sixteenth-century silk pattern.

1.

1. Wallpaper border. 2. Wallpaper design by Friedrich Fischbach.

22

Intarsia designs in the Collegio del Cambio, Perugia, ca. 1500.

Designs for linen tablecloths.

24

Intarsia ornaments from choir stalls, Elizabeth and Mary Magdalen Church, Breslau.

Intarsia ornaments.

1.

2.

3.

Marble floor mosaics. 1. From the tabernacle of Or San Michele, Florence, 1348.
2, 3. From San Martino, Lucca, 1204.

27

Borders for damask weaving.

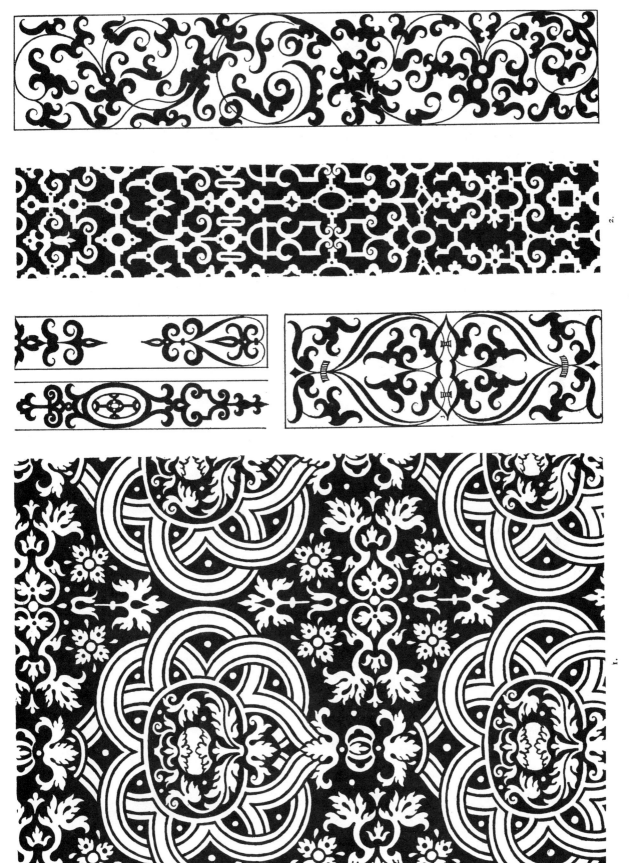

1. Ornament from a relief stone figure, St. Martin's Church, Landshut, 1570–80.
2. Marquetry ornaments from a door, Trausnitz Castle, Landshut, 1582.

Textile pattern. 2. Textile, vestment, 1480–1520.

2.

1.

Textiles, velvet on silk.

Sixteenth-century marquetry panels from choir stalls, Elizabeth and Mary Magdalen Church, Breslau.

German Renaissance flat ornament from choir stalls and the altar shrine, town church, Kamenz, Saxony.

33

Sixteenth-century damask pattern. 2. Silk pattern, 1600–60.

34

2. Bedhanging from the Castle of Ansbach, 1550–60.

1. Textile in the Holy Ghost Church, Munich.

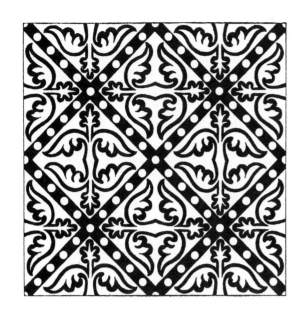

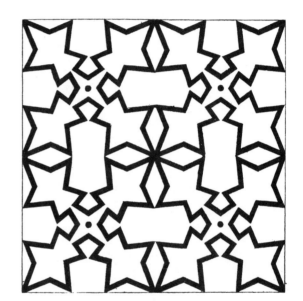

Floor tiles.

36

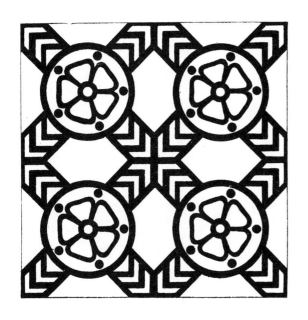

1. Textile ornament. 2. Damask pattern.

Wallpapers, of Parisian design, for the town hall, Lyons.

39

Textile designs.

Intarsia ornaments.

Intarsia ornaments, Elizabeth and Mary Magdalen Church, Breslau.

Intarsia ornaments from choir stalls, Elizabeth and Mary Magdalen Church, Breslau.

43

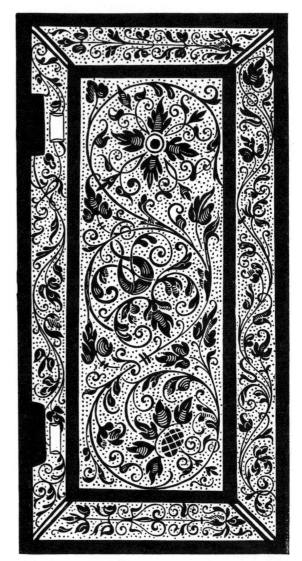

Etched ornaments from a sixteenth-century iron casket.

1. Ornament on a bronze figure in the crypt of Louis IV, the Frauenkirche, Munich, 1622. 2. Pattern carved in stone, interior, the Frauenkirche, Munich, 1560–90.

Ornaments on the inside of a sixteenth-century box.